The Principal's Journey

Navigating the Path to School Leadership

by Dr. Rachel Edoho-Eket

Copyright © 2023 by Dr. Rachel Edoho-Eket

All rights reserved. No part of this book may be reprinted or reproduced or utilized in any form or by any electronic, mechanical, or other means, now known or hereafter invented, including photocopying and recording, or in any information storage or retrieval system, without permission in writing from the publisher.

Paperback ISBN: 979-8-218-14957-4
Library of Congress Control Number: 2023902653

Cover Design, Editing & Typesetting by The VTF Publishing House (www.vtfpublishing.com)
Cover Photography by Sophia Walters Photography

ALL RIGHTS RESERVED
PRINTED IN THE USA

Dedication

To all the future leaders in education

Acknowledgements

I would like to extend my heartfelt gratitude to all those who have helped me throughout the creation of this book.

First, I would like to thank my husband, children, and extended family members for all their love and support. I have always had big dreams and I appreciate you encouraging me to go after each and every one of them!

I am deeply grateful to my cherished friends, leadership mentors, and amazing colleagues who have been my biggest cheerleaders. I have learned so much from you. Your belief, advice, and listening ear means the world to me.

I would also like to acknowledge my editor and writing coach who have played an integral role in shaping this book. Their guidance and expertise have been immeasurable.

Finally, I would like to thank my elementary school Principal, Mr. Slacum, for providing me with the inspiration to be the best school principal I can be. Your imprint is on everything I do. You have impacted me in more ways than you'll ever know.

Table of Contents

Preface 1

Chapter 1: Introduction 4
The Role of the Principal 4
The Challenges and Rewards of Being a Principal 6

Chapter 2: The Importance of a Powerful Leadership Mentor 15
Qualities of a Strong Leadership Mentor 17
Tips for Finding a Leadership Mentor 18
Sample Questions to Ask Your Leadership Mentor 19

Chapter 3: Qualifications and Requirements 27
Education and Experiences Needed to be a Principal 27
National and State Certification Requirements 28
Professional Development Opportunities 30

Chapter 4: The Hiring Process 39
Navigating the Hiring Process 39
Preparing a Strong Resume and Cover Letter 40
Interviewing Tips and Common Questions 42

Chapter 5: The First Year on the Job 52
Creating an Effective Administrative Team 54
Strategies for Building Allies and Creating a Supportive Network 56

Chapter 6: Managing the School 68
Setting Goals and Creating a Vision for the School 68
Budgeting and Financial Management 70
Curriculum and Instruction 71

Personnel Management and Teacher Evaluations 72
Discipline and Student Behavior 73

Chapter 7: Building a Positive School Culture *81*
Creating a Safe and Inclusive Environment 83
Encouraging Family and Community Involvement 84
Promoting a Culture of Learning and Excellence 85

Chapter 8: Decision Making and Navigating Hard Conversations *93*
Gaining Consensus 95
Navigating Hard Conversations 97
How to Maintain Trust After a Hard Conversation 98

Chapter 9: Time Management and Achieving a Work-Life Balance *107*
The Importance of Rest 110

Chapter 10: Conclusion *120*
Reflections on the Journey to Becoming a Principal 120
Take Opportunities as They are Presented 121
Everything is an Interview 122
The Importance of Aligning with other Strong Leaders 123
Final Words of Encouragement for Future School Leaders 124
About the Author 133

Preface

Do you want to be a principal one day? This was the life-changing question my former principal asked me almost a decade ago that changed the trajectory of my career and widened my lens to the world of school-based leadership. At the time, I was an elementary school teacher who had recently returned to work after being a stay-at-home mother to infant twins. I had just been given my first leadership opportunity as an Instructional Team Leader, and I felt I was barely keeping my head above water as I balanced my classroom responsibilities with the added responsibility of managing a large team of other teachers and support staff. When she first posed the question, my initial reaction was to quickly dismiss the suggestion and blurt out the word, "no," however, when I realized that her question was rooted in a genuine belief in my abilities, it caused me to pause and reconsider. I wondered, what did my principal see in me that I had not yet seen in myself?

In my experience as a life-long public-school educator, I continue to reflect on that simple question. In truth, I never saw myself as a future principal. I am a proud third generation educator who grew up among a family of dedicated teachers. My grandmother served as an educator in the Baltimore City Public School System for 32 years and retired as a school librarian. My mother received her college degree in music education, and my aunt retired as a music teacher from the Howard County Public School System after 30 years. As a young child, I grew up helping my grandmother and aunt set up their classrooms every year in late Summer. How I loved unpacking new learning materials together, helping to decorate colorful bulletin boards, and seeing them write lessons in their fresh planning books! After I completed my college coursework and finished my student teaching experience in the School District of Philadelphia, I was eager to have my own classroom. I have always known that my life's calling was to be a teacher and I was quite comfortable and successful in the classroom connecting with students and their families, but my principal's question continued to linger...could I have an even greater impact in my school community beyond the four walls of my classroom?

Over the course of my career, I have had the pleasure of collaborating with many different administrators, each with unique skills and talents. Working closely with my former principal was an invaluable opportunity to gain knowledge about how to effectively manage a school while also remaining authentic and approachable. As a classroom teacher, I had a limited understanding of the scope of a principal's role and responsibilities, but through learning experiences designed to stretch me as an aspiring leader, I came to understand that leadership is a continuous journey of self-discovery and improvement. Now, more than ever, there is a great need for strong and competent leaders who understand the significance of serving in this role. Our students, staff, and families are depending on kind and capable leaders who will advocate for their best interests and help them reach their highest potential. There is no greater role than to positively influence others for generations to come!

I wrote this book for anyone who is considering expanding their impact by making a transition into school-based leadership from your current position. While this book is filled with practical advice to help you as you advance in your career, it is most important to note that there are multiple pathways that exist to the principalship. In fact, every journey is different, and oftentimes the process you navigate will not be linear. My goal is to help strengthen your leadership capacity and skills to prepare you for your next role. Each chapter includes tips, suggestions, and a space for you to pause and answer reflection questions that are designed to help you determine your best course of action. Wherever you are in your career, this book is right for you. Thank you for including me as a step along your leadership journey.

Chapter One: Introduction

The Role of the Principal

The role of a principal is to provide leadership and guidance to the staff, students, and community of a school. Principals are responsible for creating and implementing policies and programs that promote student learning and success, as well as managing the day-to-day operations of the school. There are a variety of duties that a principal must undertake in order to lead a high-functioning school community. These responsibilities include:

- Building relationships with students, staff, families and the community
- Setting goals and creating a vision for the school
- Hiring high-quality, diverse staff members and evaluating programs for effectiveness
- Developing, implementing, and monitoring curriculum and instruction
- Developing and managing the school's budget
- Ensuring the safety and well-being of students, staff, and families
- Promoting a positive school culture and fostering a sense of community
- Developing and implementing policies for student behavior expectations and discipline

- Providing meaningful professional development opportunities for staff

Leadership in education is essential for creating and maintaining a successful school. A strong leader sets clear goals and communicates expectations, creates a positive and inclusive school culture, and empowers staff and students to reach their potential. In addition, effective school-based leadership is critical to student achievement, teacher satisfaction, staff retention, and community engagement. It also contributes to school safety, a positive school climate, and a culture of excellence. The role of the principal is to create an environment where teachers can teach effectively, students are engaged learners, and families are valued as educational partners. A principal should inspire and motivate all stakeholders of the school community and be a trusted ambassador for the broader school district.

When I first was promoted to the leader of my school community, I was eager to take on the role, yet understood that no one can manage all the day-to-day responsibilities alone. My goal was to help lead a school community where every student, staff member, and family is valued for the unique contributions they share with our school. Principals have a significant influence on a building's overall culture and the way we lead is critically important. To build initial connections with my teachers and staff once they returned from break, I spent most of the summer studying the school's yearbook. This simple strategy helped me to link faces with names quickly and helped me establish a positive rapport within days. In the first few weeks and months on the job, I conversed with my colleagues informally in our hallways and in their classrooms to learn more about their experiences, desires, and the personal strengths they each brought to our school. I used a journal to record notes as I listened and quickly had a good idea of areas where everyone's skills and talents could best be utilized. Some of my colleagues enjoyed using various technologies to enhance the educational experience, while others were excellent communicators and carried a large influence with our staff and community. Many teachers and support personnel were excited to contribute new ideas and engage in solution-oriented discussions to make improvements to our school and I was happy to begin to share the leadership!

The Challenges and Rewards of Being a Principal

The commitment to being a school principal encompasses both challenges and rewards. Like classroom teachers, principals must dedicate a substantial amount of time and energy to ensure that needs are met across several different areas. It is important that as you consider transitioning into the position of a school-based leader, you have a clear understanding of the complexity of the role. Some of the challenges associated with being a principal include:

- Longer working hours: Principals often work long daily hours, including evenings and weekends, to attend meetings, events, and handle emergencies as they arise.
- Increased Stress: The job of a principal can be stressful due to the many responsibilities and the additional pressure to meet school-wide academic, behavioral, and systemic goals.
- High Stakes Decision-making: Principals are responsible for making important decisions that affect the school, students, staff, and families which can be emotionally taxing.
- Conflict Management: Principals are often called upon to handle difficult conflicts between staff, students, and families.
- Balancing competing interests: Principals must balance the needs and interests of students, staff, parents, and the community, which requires strong communication and negotiation skills.

Although there are some expected challenges in the role of a school principal, I firmly believe that the benefits of serving in this role far exceed the demands. In fact, being a principal can be extremely fulfilling and offers many intrinsic rewards such as:

- Making a positive impact on students and families: Principals have the opportunity to positively impact the lives of students by providing a safe, positive, and nurturing learning environment.
- Building a strong community: Principals can build a strong and cohesive community within the school, which fosters meaningful relationships and a sense of belonging for all.
- Being a respected leader and role model: The role of a principal elevates the person to be a role model for students, staff, community members, and the education profession.
- Numerous professional growth options: The role of a principal provides many opportunities for expanding leadership experiences through attendance at administrative conferences, speaking engagements, and learning sessions.
- Making a difference: The role of a principal allows the person to make a long-lasting difference in the lives of students, staff, and the community.
- Inspiring a new generation of leaders: Principals have a strong influence on shaping future leaders and education advocates.

Reflection Questions

1. A principal performs a variety of roles and responsibilities each day. Write your top two areas of strengths and share an example of how you effectively execute these duties.

_____
_____
_____
_____
_____
_____
_____
_____
_____
_____
_____
_____
_____
_____
_____
_____
_____
_____
_____
_____

The Principal's Journey

2. Write one area of improvement that you need to develop before you transition into school-based leadership. What steps can you take to develop that area?

The Principal's Journey

3. After reviewing the challenges and rewards of being a principal, share one reward that excites you and one challenge that intimidates you. How can you plan to address the challenge to reduce its difficulty?

_____
_____
_____
_____
_____
_____
_____
_____
_____
_____
_____
_____
_____
_____
_____
_____
_____
_____
_____
_____

The Principal's Journey

Chapter Two: The Importance of a Powerful Leadership Mentor

A highly skilled leadership mentor can provide critical guidance, experiences, and support for teacher leaders who are looking to transition into school-based leadership roles. Mentors can also offer valuable insights and advice based on their own experiences. Mentors can help mentees navigate the challenges of the principalship, and act as a sounding board for ideas by providing feedback and constructive criticism. Finally, a mentor can help mentees build a network of contacts and resources that are beneficial to their personal and professional development. Overall, leadership mentors are an exceptional asset for anyone looking to grow as a leader.

One of my favorite mentors, my former principal, helped me to develop as a leader by immersing me in leadership opportunities that were designed to stretch my thinking and deepen my previous experiences. For example, she presented me with an idea to organize a school-wide end of the year event that required me to engage students, staff members, families, and community businesses. Over the course of the three months of planning, I learned how to delegate responsibilities, motivate staff volunteers towards a shared goal, create and execute a budget, use technology to communicate with a variety of stakeholders, and most importantly, problem solve using a solutions-oriented perspective. That single experience taught me several lessons that I still value to this day. Another time, she invited me to sit in on a contentious meeting with an upset parent. I sat and observed as she carefully listened to the person's concerns, offered options for rectifying the situation, and found a way to close the meeting out positively with a series of agreed upon action steps. She was able to communicate with empathy, while also sharing her distinct perspective as principal. From that experience, I learned about the importance of developing excellent communication skills and the many nuances that can influence challenging situations and decisions.

I am fortunate to have had several wonderful mentors throughout my professional career. My most powerful mentors helped me to set attainable goals and provide a level of accountability to ensure that I stay focused and on track. One of the main components of a successful mentor/mentee relationship is mutual trust and respect. Skilled mentors have the ability to challenge, inspire confidence, and reassure developing leaders as they take risks and navigate unfamiliar experiences. They are the key to fortifying your leadership.

Qualities of a Strong Leadership Mentor

A strong principal mentor should possess several key qualities, including:

- Strong leadership skills: The ability to lead by example and provide guidance and direction to others.
- Excellent communication skills: Strong mentors possess the capacity to effectively communicate with teachers, staff, students, and parents.
- A deep understanding of instruction: A strong principal mentor should have a deep understanding of teaching and learning and be able to provide support to teachers in their professional development.
- A willingness to collaborate: A good principal mentor should be open to working with others and be willing to collaborate with other stakeholders to achieve common goals.
- Possess cultural competence: A dedicated mentor should be culturally competent and be able to work with diverse groups of people.
- A commitment to continuous improvement: An effective mentor should be dedicated to continuous improvement and be willing to reflect on their own practice and make changes as needed.
- An in-depth understanding of the community: A mentor should have a deep understanding of the

community they serve and be able to work with families and other community members to support student success.
- A good listener: A strong principal mentor should be a good listener and be able to give thoughtful feedback.
- Empathetic: A mentor should be empathetic and understand the challenges that teachers, staff, students, and families face.

Tips for Finding a Leadership Mentor

If you have not identified a leadership mentor, consider using these tips below:

- Be proactive: Don't wait for a mentor to come to you, take the initiative to reach out and make connections.
- Network: Reach out to colleagues, supervisors, or professional organizations to ask for recommendations of potential mentors.
- Look for someone with experience: A mentor who has experience as a principal or in a similar leadership role will be better equipped to provide guidance and support.
- Consider compatibility: It's important to find a mentor whose leadership style, values, and goals align with your own.

- Do your research: Research potential mentors by reading their publications, articles, or attending their professional development session.
- Ask for an interview: Reach out to potential mentors and ask if they are willing to meet with you for an informal interview.
- Be prepared: Come to the mentorship meeting with specific goals and outcomes.

Sample Questions to Ask your Leadership Mentor

When seeking guidance from a leadership mentor, it can be helpful to ask specific questions to gain valuable insights and advice. Some potential questions to consider asking include:

- How do you approach decision making and problem solving?
- How do you handle difficult conversations and conflicts?
- How do you prioritize and manage your time effectively?
- How do you build and maintain effective teams?
- How do you handle stress and maintain work-life balance?
- How do you handle criticism and feedback?
- How do you inspire and motivate others?
- How do you handle change?

- How do you build and maintain a positive culture and work environment?
- Can you share a specific example of a leadership challenge you faced and how you overcame it?

Remember to tailor these questions to your specific needs and goals as an aspiring leader and ask follow-up questions to gain more detailed information.

Reflection Questions

1. Write the names of 2-3 mentors in your organization who can help you reach your leadership goals. What qualities do they possess that you want to develop in yourself?

_____
_____
_____
_____
_____
_____
_____
_____
_____
_____
_____
_____
_____
_____
_____
_____
_____
_____

The Principal's Journey

2. If you currently do not have a high-quality leadership mentor, what strategies will you use to acquire one? Create a plan to start the process.

_____
_____
_____
_____
_____
_____
_____
_____
_____
_____
_____
_____
_____
_____
_____
_____
_____
_____
_____
_____
_____
_____

The Principal's Journey

3. List 3 new experiences you want to explore with a mentor to strengthen your leadership journey.

The Principal's Journey

Chapter Three: Qualifications and Requirements

Education and Experiences Needed to Become a Principal

The education and experience required to become a principal varies by each state and individual school district, however, most states and districts require that principals have a master's degree in education (or a related field) and have several years of experience as a teacher or administrator.

Typically, to become a principal, one would need:

- A bachelor's degree in education or a related field
- A master's degree in education administration or a related field
- Several years of experience as a teacher or administrator
- State certification or licensure as a school administrator

A master's degree in education administration or a related field is usually required. These degree programs usually include courses in educational leadership, curriculum development, and school management. Principals need to have a good understanding of the day-to-day operations of a school and the needs of students, staff, and families. This experience is best gained through working as a teacher, assistant principal, or central office administrator before becoming a principal. A state certification or licensure as a school administrator is also required by most jurisdictions. This certification is usually obtained by passing a standardized test and completing a certain number of professional development or field experience hours in preparation for the role. It's important to check the specific requirements for your state and school district, as they can vary.

National and State Certification Requirements

Most states require that principals hold state certification or licensure as a school administrator. The certification exam tests the candidate's knowledge of educational leadership, school management, and state laws and regulations. Continuing education is also required to maintain certification. This typically involves taking professional development courses to stay current on education trends and best practices, as well as to renew the certification every few years. There are also additional certification programs and memberships available, such as the National Board for Professional Teaching Standards, the National Association of Elementary School Principals, the National Association of Secondary School Principals, and National Board Standards for Accomplished Principals. Although these memberships and additional certifications are not mandatory, they are recognized and respected by many schools and districts across the United States. These certifications are based on rigorous standards and indicate that the candidate has met the highest level of professional development and expertise in their field.

As you are considering your current education and certification needs towards becoming a school-based leader, I encourage you to first reach out to your district's certification office to determine what additional requirements you need to acquire for the role. In my experience, districts can often perform "credit audits" to help you reach your certification goals even faster. During a credit audit, certification departments examine your previous educational transcripts to see where credits can be transferred and added towards your credential requirements. This is an excellent way to save a tremendous amount of time and money!

When I first began my Master's program over 15 years ago, I had a choice to focus solely on Curriculum and Instruction as a specialized area or Curriculum and Instruction with an additional component of the Administration Certification. The latter program was slightly longer because it included an internship experience, and at the time, I did not have aspirations to become a school-based leader so I did not choose that program. In hindsight, I should have chosen the slightly longer Master's program because I would not have had to return to graduate school years later to complete my Administrator 1 certifications coursework separately. It is my recommendation that any teacher or aspiring leader complete the coursework for an Administration Certification even if you are unsure of your future career steps. It is important to note that some educational positions require you to obtain an Administrator certification before you can be considered for the job, so it is critical that you are eligible for as many positions as possible.

Professional Development Opportunities

Professional development opportunities for principals are important to enhance their knowledge, skills and abilities to lead and manage a school effectively. Some examples of professional development opportunities for principals include:

- Conferences and workshops: Many professional organizations and education groups offer conferences and workshops for principals on a variety of topics, such as curriculum development, school safety, and leadership skills.
- Online courses and webinars: There are many online courses and webinars that principals can take to learn

about new education policies, best practices, and leadership strategies.

- Mentoring and coaching: Principals can benefit from mentoring and coaching programs, where they can work with experienced administrators to improve their skills and knowledge.
- Advanced degrees and certifications: Principals can pursue advanced degrees, such as an Ed. D or Ph. D in Educational leadership, or additional certifications, such as the National Board for Professional Teaching Standards to advance their careers and increase their knowledge and skills.
- Professional organizations and associations: Joining professional organizations and associations for school administrators can provide opportunities for networking, sharing ideas and best practices, and staying current with education trends and policies.
- On-the-job learning: Many schools and districts provide opportunities for principals to observe and learn from other successful leaders, to participate in school improvement teams, or to take on additional responsibilities to gain new skills and experience.

Professional development is an ongoing process, and it is important for principals to continuously seek out opportunities to improve and stay current in their field. By taking advantage of the various professional development opportunities available, principals can increase their knowledge, skills, and effectiveness as a leader, which has a positive impact on the school community and the students they serve.

Reflection Questions

1. In your current role as a teacher or school-based leader, what experiences do you have that would make your transition to the principalship successful?

The Principal's Journey

2. Review your current educational coursework and certifications. Which courses and certifications are you most interested in completing? Record a timeline for completion.

_____
_____
_____
_____
_____
_____
_____
_____
_____
_____
_____
_____
_____
_____
_____
_____
_____
_____
_____
_____

The Principal's Journey

3. Consider what professional development opportunities best meet your current needs. Research options and write two opportunities that will help you grow as a leader.

_____
_____
_____
_____
_____
_____
_____
_____
_____
_____
_____
_____
_____
_____
_____
_____
_____
_____
_____
_____

The Principal's Journey

Chapter Four: The Hiring Process

Navigating the Hiring Process

The next step in your leadership journey is an exciting one. Once you make the decision to formally apply for a school-based leadership position, it typically involves several steps:

- Job posting: The school district or hiring committee will create a job posting, which will be advertised on the district website and/or local/state professional organizations.
- Resume and application review: Candidates will submit resumes and applications, which will be reviewed by a hiring committee or district administrators to ensure that they meet the minimum qualifications for the position.
- Interviews: Selected candidates will be interviewed by the hiring committee or district administrators. The interviews may be done in person, over the phone, or through video conferencing. It is also important to note that schools and districts may have additional requirements or steps in the hiring process, such as assessments, simulations or presentations. Additionally, some districts may also involve parents, teachers or students in the hiring selection process.

- Reference and background check: Candidates will be asked to provide professional references, and the hiring committee will conduct background checks to verify the candidate's qualifications and ensure the safety of the students and staff.
- Decision-making: The hiring committee or district administrators will review the resumes, applications, interviews, and reference checks, and make a final decision on the candidate to be offered the position.
- Offer and acceptance: The candidate will be offered the position, and if they accept, they will be required to complete any necessary paperwork before starting the position.

Preparing a Strong Resume and Cover Letter

Preparing a resume and cover letter for a school-based leadership position is a critical step for showcasing your qualifications, experiences, and skills and distinguishes yourself as a strong candidate. It is very important to keep your resume up to date. In my experience, the easiest way to keep your resume current is to update it each time you have a significant leadership opportunity or experience. For instance, if you lead a professional development session, serve on a panel, organize a parent engagement activity, etc. you should add it to your resume as soon as you finish. Over time, you will have an excellent record of your unique skills and talents that you can polish and refine later.

Here are some tips for preparing a strong resume and cover letter:

- Tailor your resume and cover letter to the specific position and job description: This means researching the school district and the position to which you are applying and highlighting how your qualifications, experiences, and skills align with the specific needs of the district and the position.
- Highlight your education and experience in education administration: Make sure to include your education and experience in administration, including your degrees, certifications, and any relevant coursework.
- Emphasize your leadership experience: Highlight any leadership experience you have, such as experience as a teacher leader, department head, mentor, or administrator.
- Include any relevant experiences, skills, and accomplishments: Include experiences, skills, and accomplishments that demonstrate your ability to lead and manage a school, such as experience with curriculum development, budget management, or parent and community engagement.

- Keep it concise and well-organized: Keep your resume and cover letter concise and well-organized, using bullet points and clear, easy-to-read formatting.
- Proofread and edit: Carefully proofread and edit your resume and cover letter to ensure that they are error-free.
- Address any concerns or qualifications gaps: In your cover letter, address any concerns or qualifications gaps that the hiring committee or district administrators may have.

Interviewing Tips and Common Questions

The interview process for an administrative position is an important step in the hiring process. It allows the hiring committee or district administrators to assess your qualifications, experiences, and skills and determine if you are the best fit for the position. These are some helpful tips to help prepare for an interview and some common questions you might expect:

- Research the school district and the position: Research the school district and the position to which you are applying and be prepared to discuss how your qualifications, experiences, and skills align with the needs of the district and the position.

- Practice your responses: Practice your responses to common interview questions and have specific examples ready to share. Include how you will address students, staff, and families in each answer to make it more comprehensive.
- Dress professionally and arrive on time for the interview.
- Prepare to discuss your experience working with diverse populations and how you will promote equity and inclusion in the school.
- Communicate your leadership style: Be prepared to discuss your leadership style, what you believe makes an effective leader, and how you handle difficult situations.
- Share your experience with data-driven decision making and how you will use data to inform instruction and improve student achievement.
- Describe your vision for the school and your goals for improving student achievement.
- Show enthusiasm and passion: Demonstrate your eagerness for the position and the school district during the interview.

Here are some common questions you might expect during an interview. Remember to make your responses as comprehensive as possible by including information on how you will address staff, students, and families. Additionally, one meaningful example that directly relates to the question and highlights your leadership expertise should always be included in your answer, so the panel has a clear picture of the leader you are.

- How do you involve parents and the community in the school?
- How do you promote equity and inclusion in the school?
- Describe a time you handled a difficult situation. What did you learn?
- How do you use data to improve student achievement for targeted student groups?
- Can you describe a successful project or initiative you have led in the past?
- How do you handle staff evaluations and evaluations of their performance?
- How do you handle budget and financial management?
- How do you handle discipline and student behavior?
- How do you foster a positive and inclusive school culture?
- Can you describe a time when you had to make a difficult decision and how you handled it?

- What are your goals for the school and how do you plan to achieve them?

These are some common questions that you might expect during an interview for a school-based leadership position, but it's important to keep in mind that the questions may vary depending on the district and the position. It's also important to be prepared to answer follow-up questions the interviewers may have.

Reflection Questions

1. In considering the hiring process, what area(s) do you think you are most prepared for and what area(s) do you need to work on?

_____
_____
_____
_____
_____
_____
_____
_____
_____
_____
_____
_____
_____
_____
_____
_____
_____
_____
_____

Dr. Rachel Edoho-Eket

2. When was the last time you updated your resume and cover letter to reflect your current leadership journey? Write down a plan that includes a date/time to work on these two items.

_____
_____
_____
_____
_____
_____
_____
_____
_____
_____
_____
_____
_____
_____
_____
_____
_____
_____
_____
_____

Dr. Rachel Edoho-Eket

3. Review the sample interview questions. Record three questions you are struggling to adequately answer and brainstorm additional leadership experiences you can do to address these gaps.

Chapter Five: The First Year on the Job

The first year on the job as an administrator can be a challenging yet rewarding experience. Principals are responsible for providing leadership and guidance to the staff, students, and community of a school. They are also responsible for creating and implementing policies and programs that promote student learning and success, as well as managing the day-to-day operations of the school. During the first year, a new administrator should focus on the following:

- Building relationships: Building positive relationships with staff, students, parents, and community members is essential to the success of a school. A new school-based leader should take the time to get to know the staff and students and build trust and respect with the community.
- Assessing the school's needs: A new principal should assess the school's needs and strengths and create a plan to address areas for improvement. This can include conducting surveys or facilitating discussion groups, analyzing data, and gathering feedback from the staff, students, and community.
- Developing a vision and goals: Administrators should develop a vision and goals for the school and work

with the staff to create a plan to achieve them. This can include setting academic and organizational goals, as well as creating a plan for professional development.
- Fostering a positive school culture: Fostering a positive and inclusive school culture is essential to the success of a school. Administrators should work with the staff to create a positive school culture that promotes student learning and success and encourages the staff to work together as a team.
- Ensuring the safety and well-being of students and staff: A new principal should ensure that the school is a safe and healthy environment for students and staff. This can include implementing policies and procedures for crisis management, emergency preparedness, and school security.
- Communicating effectively: Effective communication is essential for a principal. It should be clear and consistent and involve all the stakeholders of the school.

In the first few years, a new principal will be learning and adapting to the school culture, students, staff, and the community. It can take some time to adjust and become comfortable in the role, but by focusing on building relationships, assessing the school's needs, developing a vision and goals, fostering a positive school culture, and communicating effectively, the new leader will be well on their way to success.

Creating an Effective Administrative Team

Collaborating with your Assistant Principal is an important responsibility of school leaders. Assistant Principals (APs) play a critical role in supporting principals in managing and leading the school and can provide valuable support in areas such as curriculum development, instruction, student behavior and discipline, and professional development. Shared leadership between the principal and AP involves working together to create and implement school policies, procedures, and programs that support student learning and academic achievement. It can also involve sharing responsibilities and delegating tasks, such as observing and evaluating teachers, and providing feedback and support to improve their instruction.

In the best leadership teams, principals and APs work together to create a positive and inclusive school culture and promote a safe and secure learning environment for all students. This includes developing and implementing policies and procedures that promote positive student behavior, and addressing any issues related to discrimination and bias. For the collaboration to be effective, there must be clear lines of communication and trust between the principal and AP including regular meetings to discuss school-wide related issues and plans, as well as open lines of communication for sharing ideas and seeking feedback. Collaborating with your Assistant Principal is an essential responsibility of school principals, as it can provide valuable support in managing and leading the school and can help to improve student learning and academic achievement.

Creating a strong administrative team involves several key steps:

- Clearly define the roles and responsibilities of each leader.
- Establishing clear lines of communication and fostering a culture of collaboration and teamwork.
- Committing to a designated administrative team weekly meeting date/time
- Providing ongoing training and development opportunities to ensure that the team can effectively perform their duties.
- Regularly evaluating and assessing the performance of the admin team and providing feedback and action steps for improvement.
- Ensuring that the team has the necessary resources and support to effectively carry out their duties.

- Building a positive and supportive work environment where team members feel valued and motivated to perform at their best.

Strategies for Building Allies and Creating a Supportive Network

Building a positive relationship with staff involves fostering a culture of trust, respect, and open communication. This can be achieved through clear and consistent communication, recognizing and rewarding good work, providing opportunities for professional development and growth, and actively listening to and addressing staff concerns. Additionally, creating a positive work environment by promoting work-life balance and creating a sense of community and team spirit can also help to build positive relationships with staff. Principals can build relationships with staff by:

- Get to know teachers: Take the time to get to know the staff members, their interests, and their skills through informal conversations, surveys, or other means.
- Communicate clearly and consistently: Regularly communicate with staff and ensure that information is accurate and timely. This helps to build trust and keep staff informed about important developments.

- Recognize and reward good work: Show appreciation for staff's contributions and efforts and recognize their achievements. This helps to boost morale and motivation.
- Provide opportunities for professional development: Invest in the professional development of staff members, by providing training, mentorship, and networking opportunities. Aspiring teacher leaders should also lead professional learning for staff.
- Listen to and address staff concerns: Actively listen to staff's concerns and feedback and take appropriate action to address them. This helps to build trust.
- Create a positive work environment: Promote work-life balance, encourage a healthy work culture, and create a sense of community and team spirit. This helps to foster a positive and productive work environment.
- Lead by example: Lead by example in all aspects of your work, including communication, teamwork, and ethical behavior. This establishes credibility with staff members.
- Encourage open communication: Encourage open communication and provide a safe environment for employees to share their ideas, feedback, and concerns.
- Be available and approachable: Make yourself available and approachable to your staff and

encourage them to come to you with any questions or concerns they may have.
- Create a sense of community: Encourage team-building activities, celebrate successes, and create a sense of community among staff members.

Building positive relationships with students involves creating a safe and inclusive environment, actively listening to and valuing their perspectives, providing clear and consistent communication, setting clear expectations and boundaries, and consistently treating them with respect and kindness. It also includes providing opportunities for students to take ownership of their learning and providing positive feedback and recognition for their efforts and achievements. Tips for fostering good relationships with students include:

- Learn student's names and pronounce them correctly: A person's name is one of the most valuable parts of their identity. Invest the time to learn names quickly using mnemonics and associations to remember.
- Be approachable: Make yourself available to students and let them know that they can come to you with any concerns or questions.
- Show interest in their lives: Ask about their families, hobbies, and extracurricular activities. Showing an

interest in their lives outside of the classroom helps to create a positive connection.

- Provide positive feedback: Recognize and acknowledge student's efforts, progress, and achievements. This helps to build their confidence and self-esteem.
- Set clear boundaries: Establish clear expectations for behavior and communication. This helps students understand what is and isn't acceptable and promotes a positive learning environment.
- Encourage participation: Provide opportunities for students to actively participate in the school. This helps them feel more engaged and invested in the learning process.
- Be consistent: Treat all students fairly and consistently. This creates a sense of trust and respect.
- Be a good listener: Listen actively to students and take their perspectives into account. This helps them feel heard and valued.
- Create a safe space: Create a school environment that is safe, inclusive, and respectful of all students.
- Lead by example: Model the behavior and attitudes you want to see in your students.

Fostering positive relationships with families involves clear and consistent communication, valuing and utilizing their input and involvement, being accessible and responsive, and building trust and mutual respect. Here are some tips to help foster positive relationships with parents:

- Communicate regularly: Keep parents informed about their child's progress, behavior, and any relevant information about the class or school. Use a variety of communication methods such as email, phone, and in-person or video conferences.
- Involve parents: Encourage and welcome parent involvement in the classroom and school. This can be done through volunteering, attending events, and participating in decision-making processes.
- Be accessible: Make sure parents know how to reach you and have a clear understanding of your availability.
- Listen and respond: Be open to feedback and suggestions from parents. Listen actively and respond in a timely and respectful manner.
- Build trust: Be transparent and honest with parents about their child's progress, strengths, and areas for improvement.
- Show appreciation: Show appreciation for the time and effort that parents put into their child's education. Recognize and acknowledge their contributions.

- Be respectful: Show respect for the diversity of families and cultures represented in the school.
- Build a relationship: Take the time to get to know each family and their unique needs and concerns. Building a relationship with parents will make communication and problem-solving easier in the future.
- Partner up: work together with parents to set goals and develop a plan to help their child succeed.
- Be positive: maintain a positive attitude and approach towards the parents and the students, it helps to build a positive relationship.

It's important to remember that building relationships with staff, students, and families takes time and effort, but it is an important investment for the success of the school and its community. It is also important to be responsive and respectful to the needs and concerns of all stakeholders.

Reflection Questions

1. List examples of the powerful ways you currently connect with your colleagues. How will this influence how you lead as an administrator?

_____
_____
_____
_____
_____
_____
_____
_____
_____
_____
_____
_____
_____
_____
_____
_____
_____
_____
_____
_____

Dr. Rachel Edoho-Eket

2. Write an example of the strongest connection you have ever had with a student. As principal, how can you expand similar connections school-wide?

3. Describe a time that you had a challenging situation with a family. What did you learn from that experience?

Dr. Rachel Edoho-Eket

Chapter Six: Managing the School

Effective school management is critical to the success of a school. Principals are responsible for setting the vision, mission, and goals of the school, creating a positive and safe learning environment, and ensuring that teachers and staff have the resources and support they need to help students achieve academic success. They also play a key role in developing and implementing policies and procedures that promote student achievement, as well as managing the budget, facilities, and other resources of the school. In short, effective school management by principals is essential to creating a positive and successful learning environment for students.

Setting Goals and Creating a Vision for the School

Setting goals and creating a vision for the school is an important task for school-based leaders. It helps to establish direction, focus, and purpose for the school community, and serves as a roadmap for achieving success. Here are some tips for setting goals and creating a vision for the school:

- Involve the school community: Include the school community in the process of setting goals and creating a shared vision. This can include staff, students, parents, and community members. Input from the

community can help to ensure that the goals and vision align with their needs and priorities, and increases collective buy in.
- Analyze data: Examine all data sources related to the school's academic performance, attendance, and student demographics. This can help to identify areas of strength and areas that need improvement, and to set goals that are aligned with the school's needs.
- Establish clear, measurable, and achievable goals: The goals should be specific, measurable, attainable, relevant and time-bound (SMART)
- Create a plan: Identify a plan that includes specific strategies, assigns responsibilities, and establishes timelines for achieving the goals.
- Communicate the goals and vision: Share the goals and vision to the school community and ensure that everyone is aware of their role in achieving the goals.
- Monitor progress and adjust as needed: This can include reviewing data, seeking feedback, and making adjustments to the plan to ensure that the goals are being met.
- Celebrate successes: Establish regular checkpoints and recognize the efforts of the school community in achieving the goals.

Budgeting and Financial Management

Budgeting and financial management are important responsibilities of school principals. They are responsible for creating and managing the school's budget, which includes allocating funds for things like textbooks and classroom materials. They must also ensure that the school's finances are being used effectively and efficiently to support the school's academic mission and goals. The principal is responsible for monitoring spending, and making sure that the school is following all financial regulations and laws. School-based leaders should be prepared to advocate with stakeholders when necessary to ensure that the school has adequate funding to meet its needs, and that any surplus funds are invested in ways that will benefit the school in the long term.

In addition to budgeting and financial management, principals must also be able to communicate effectively with school district officials, parents and community members about the school's budget and financial status. This includes being able to explain the school's budget and how it is being used to support student achievement. Budgeting and financial management are critical responsibilities of school leaders, as they play a key role in ensuring that schools have the resources needed to provide high-quality education to students.

Curriculum and Instruction

Extensive knowledge of curriculum and instruction are key responsibilities of school principals. Principals are responsible for creating and implementing academic programs that align with the district's vision, mission, and goals, and that meet the needs of all students. This may include selecting and adopting appropriate curriculum materials, as well as developing and implementing instructional strategies that are needed for teaching the curriculum. Principals also play a critical role in evaluating the effectiveness of the curriculum and instruction. This includes evaluating teacher instruction, monitoring student progress, analyzing assessment scores and other data, and using this information to make decisions about what modifications are needed to improve student achievement.

In addition, school-based leaders are responsible for providing professional development opportunities for teachers to improve their instructional skills and stay current with best practices. They also must be able to communicate effectively with parents and other stakeholders about the school's curriculum and be able to explain how it supports student achievement. In summary, curriculum and instruction are major responsibilities of school principals, as they play a critical role in ensuring that students are receiving a high-quality education that meets their needs and prepares them for success in their future academic and career pursuits.

Personnel Management and Teacher Evaluations

Personnel management and teacher evaluation processes are an important role of school principals. Leaders are responsible for managing the school's staff, which includes hiring, supervising, and evaluating teachers, support staff, and other service providers. In terms of personnel management, principals must ensure that the school has enough qualified staff members to meet the needs of students. They must also be able to create and maintain a positive and supportive work environment, and to resolve any conflicts or issues that may arise to help overall morale.

With respect to evaluations, principals are responsible for regularly assessing the performance of teachers and staff members. This includes monitoring their work and providing feedback, as well as conducting formal and informal evaluations that are used to determine their effectiveness and identify areas for improvement. The evaluations are also used to support staff development and inform decisions about additional leadership opportunities, transfers, and other personnel actions. Principals must be able to communicate effectively with teachers, staff and district officials about personnel matters and evaluations, and be able to explain how evaluations are used to support the school's mission and goals and to promote student achievement. In short, personnel management and evaluations are essential responsibilities of school principals, as they play a key role in ensuring that the school has a high-quality and effective staff, and that the staff is supported in their efforts to improve student achievement.

Discipline and Student Behavior

Principals are responsible for creating and implementing policies and procedures that promote positive student behavior and a safe and orderly learning environment. This includes developing and enforcing expectations for behavior, as well as providing support and resources for students who may be struggling with various behavioral issues. Within the past few years, some school districts have adopted restorative practices within their student code of conduct policies and procedures in an effort to increase build positive relationships and reduce, prevent, and minimize harmful behavior.

One of the key roles of the principal is to ensure that student discipline is applied in a fair and consistent manner. They should also be able to handle and resolve conflicts and crises that may arise in the school. In addition, school-based leaders must be prepared to work collaboratively with teachers, counselors, and other staff members to identify and address the underlying causes of student misbehavior, and to provide support and resources to help students develop positive behavior and social-emotional skills. It is best if a school-wide system of discipline expectations and procedures is shared with all stakeholders in the school community to increase transparency and understanding. Principals also must communicate effectively with parents, students, and staff about discipline and student behavior, and be able to explain how the school's policies and procedures promote positive student behaviors. In short, managing discipline and student behavior are important responsibilities of school principals, as they play a critical role in creating a positive and safe learning environment for students while promoting student success.

Reflection Questions

1. As an inspiring leader, what are some strategies you would use to include all stakeholders in creating a shared vision for your school?

_____
_____
_____
_____
_____
_____
_____
_____
_____
_____
_____
_____
_____
_____
_____
_____
_____

The Principal's Journey

2. Which of the following three areas do you need additional leadership experience with? For example, budgeting, curriculum/instruction, or managing personnel/evaluations. What actions can you take to ensure professional learning occurs for you?

_____

_____

_____

_____

_____

_____

_____

_____

_____

_____

_____

_____

_____

_____

_____

_____

_____

_____

_____

The Principal's Journey

3. Describe how you will promote positive student behaviors in your school and how you plan to address student misbehavior fairly and consistently.

The Principal's Journey

Dr. Rachel Edoho-Eket

Chapter Seven: Building a Positive School Culture

Building a positive school culture is central to the work of school principals. A positive school culture is one in which all members of the school community feel valued, respected, and supported, and where academic excellence and student success are emphasized. School-based leaders play a key role in creating and maintaining a positive school culture by setting a vision and mission that aligns with the school's values, and by promoting positive relationships among students, staff, families, and the broader community. This includes encouraging frequent communication, collaboration, and teamwork among all members of the school community.

Administrators also play an important part in creating a sense of belonging, ownership, and pride in the school. This can be achieved by involving students, staff and community members in decision-making processes, recognizing and celebrating achievements, and fostering a sense of camaraderie through special events and activities. In addition, principals should also be able to promote a safe and inclusive learning environment for all students, regardless of their background or abilities. This comprises implementing policies and practices that promote diversity, equity, inclusion, respect, and understanding. Principals must also be able to communicate effectively with all members of the school community about the school culture and be able to explain how it supports student success. In essence, building a positive school culture is a critical responsibility of school-based administrators, as it plays a strong role in promoting academic excellence, student success, and a sense of community among all stakeholders in the school community.

Here are some additional tips for building a positive school culture:

- Recognize and reward positive behavior and accomplishments.
- Provide opportunities for student voice and leadership.
- Involve parents and families in the life of the school.
- Continuously evaluate and improve the school culture through surveys, focus groups, and other forms of feedback.
- Clearly define and communicate expectations for behavior and academic performance.
- Encourage positive relationships among students and staff through opportunities for collaboration and teamwork.
- Promote a sense of belonging and inclusivity for all students.

- Encourage open communication and active listening among all members of the school community.

Creating a Safe and Inclusive Environment

A safe and inclusive environment is one in which all students feel physically and emotionally safe, and where all students are respected, valued, and included. Principals play a strong role in creating a safe and inclusive environment by developing and implementing policies and procedures that promote safety and security, as well as those that address discrimination and bias. This includes abiding by a student code of conduct that clearly defines acceptable behavior and establishes equitable consequences for violating it. They should also be able to ensure that the school is physically safe and secure, by implementing emergency plans and conducting regular safety drills with staff and students.

School-based leaders should promote inclusivity and equity within their schools by implementing policies and practices that promote acceptance of a diverse student body, multiple perspectives, and varied learning experiences. This encompasses creating an environment where all students feel welcome, valued, and supported, and where they can be their authentic selves. Principals must also be able to communicate effectively with all members of the school community about the school's policies and practices related to inclusion and be able to explain how they support the well-being of all students and the academic mission of the school. Creating a safe and inclusive environment is a critical responsibility of school principals, as it plays a key role in promoting student belonging, academic success, and fostering a positive and inclusive school culture.

Encouraging Family and Community Involvement

Actively involved parents and highly engaged community members are the cornerstone of successful schools. Parent involvement plays a significant part in supporting student progress and promoting a positive and inclusive school culture. Principals play a large role in encouraging parent and community involvement by building strong relationships with families and community members, and by communicating effectively with them about the school's mission, goals, and programs. This includes actively seeking out and responding to feedback from parents and community members and involving them in decision-making processes.

Administrators can also encourage parent and community involvement by creating opportunities for parents and community members to volunteer and participate in school activities, such as parent-teacher conferences, school events, and volunteer opportunities. They should also be able to provide regular updates and information about the school to parents and community members through various channels, such as newsletters, emails, and social media. Principals must also be able to collaborate with community organizations and agencies to provide additional support and resources to students and families, such as mentoring programs, after-school activities, and other enrichment opportunities. In short, encouraging parent and community involvement is a critical responsibility of school principals, as it plays a key role in promoting student success, building strong relationships with families and community members, and fostering a positive and inclusive school culture.

Promoting a Culture of Learning and Excellence

Promoting a culture of learning and excellence is an important responsibility of school-based leaders. A culture of learning and excellence is one in which academic achievement is highly valued, and where students, teachers, and staff are continuously working to improve and excel in their respective areas. Principals must create a culture of learning and excellence by setting high expectations for academic achievement and creating a positive and supportive learning environment. This includes clearly communicating the school's academic goals and expectations to students, staff, and parents, and monitoring and assessing student progress to ensure that they are meeting these goals.

School-based administrators also play a role in promoting a culture of learning and excellence by providing professional development opportunities for teachers and staff to improve their instructional skills and stay current with best practices in education. Aspiring teacher leaders should have the opportunity to present professional learning sessions to their peers, as this often promotes higher engagement among colleagues, and deepens the leadership experience of future leaders. Administrators should also recognize and reward academic achievement and excellence by creating opportunities for students to showcase their work, and by providing recognition and incentives for students.

Principals must communicate frequently with all members of the school community about the school's culture of learning and excellence and be able to explain how it supports student success and academic achievement. Promoting a culture of learning and excellence is a critical responsibility of school principals, as it plays a key role in setting high expectations for academic achievement, fostering a positive and supportive learning environment and encouraging continuous improvement among students, teachers and staff.

Reflection Questions

1. List some ways that you promote belonging, ownership, and pride in your school. As principal, what other people or resources can you use to help all students feel valued?

_____
_____
_____
_____
_____
_____
_____
_____
_____
_____
_____
_____
_____
_____
_____
_____
_____
_____
_____
_____

The Principal's Journey

2. At your current school, are parents involved in any decision-making processes? If so, how? If not, how can you help parents play a role in decisions impacting the school?

_____
_____
_____
_____
_____
_____
_____
_____
_____
_____
_____
_____
_____
_____
_____
_____
_____
_____
_____
_____

The Principal's Journey

3. Staff members are often more receptive to professional development when their colleagues present the information. What professional learning would you present to staff if given an opportunity? List your ideas below and create a plan to do the actual presentation.

The Principal's Journey

Chapter Eight: Decision Making and Navigating Hard Conversations

Good decision making in schools is crucial as it affects students, staff, and families in the community. It impacts students' academic and personal growth, shapes the school culture and environment, and determines the allocation of resources. Effective decision making can lead to positive outcomes such as improved student performance, increased teacher morale, and an enhanced school reputation. On the other hand, poor decisions can result in low staff morale, decreased academic achievement, and a negative school image. Therefore, it is important for school-based leaders to increase their decision-making skills to ensure the best possible outcomes for staff, students, and parents.

Decision making is the process of identifying and choosing a course of action from multiple options. Effective decision making is important for achieving goals and success in any organization. Some key elements of effective decision making include:

- Clearly define the problem or decision that needs to be made.
- Gathering and analyzing relevant information.
- Generating potential solutions or options.

- Evaluating and comparing the potential options and their possible outcomes.
- Choosing the best course of action.
- Implementing the decision and monitoring its effectiveness.

Deciding when decisions are urgent or can be delayed requires careful consideration of various factors. Here are some factors to consider as you are faced with making key decisions as principal:

- Impact on students: Decisions that affect the immediate safety of students and staff should be made urgently.
- Time sensitivity: Decisions that have a deadline or time-sensitive components should be prioritized.
- Resources: Decisions that involve the allocation of limited resources should be made promptly.
- Stakeholder involvement: Decisions that require the input of multiple stakeholders should be made in a timely manner to ensure their active participation.
- Long-term effects: Decisions that have a significant impact on the school in the long term should be given careful consideration and prioritized accordingly.

It is important to strike a balance between the urgency of a decision and the time needed to make an informed and thoughtful decision. Leaders should prioritize decisions that have a direct impact on the well-being and education of students, while also considering other factors such as time sensitivity and resource allocation. Additionally, it's important to involve the right people in the decision-making process and consider different perspectives, values, and needs of the stakeholders.

Gaining Consensus

Gaining consensus among staff, students, and families requires a proactive and inclusive approach. Here are some ways to gain consensus:

- Clearly define the issue and desired outcome.
- Involve all relevant stakeholders, including administrators, teachers, students, and parents.
- Encourage open and honest communication.
- Listen actively to all perspectives and ideas.
- Seek common ground and prioritize shared values.
- Identify and address any objections or concerns.
- Use a decision-making method that is fair and transparent.
- Develop a clear and agreed upon plan of action.

At times, a full consensus may not be able to be reached. Finalizing a decision when others disagree can be challenging for administrators, but it's important to approach the situation with empathy and professionalism. Here are some steps to consider:

- Re-evaluate the decision: Consider if there is new information that could change the decision.
- Address concerns: Listen to the objections and address them in a constructive manner.
- Find common ground: Seek a solution that aligns with shared values and priorities.
- Consider alternative options: Explore different approaches to see if there is a mutually acceptable solution.
- Make a final decision: If a consensus cannot be reached, make a decision based on what is in the best interest of the school community.

It is important to communicate the decision and the reasoning behind it clearly to all stakeholders once the decision has been made. If necessary, provide a clear plan of action for how to move forward and address any remaining concerns. By following these steps, principals can ensure that decisions are made in a fair and transparent manner, even in the face of disagreement. Using these methods, all stakeholders can work together to achieve a mutually beneficial solution. It is important to keep in mind that the process of gaining consensus may take time and patience, but ultimately it leads to better decision-making and a more cohesive and effective school community.

Navigating Hard Conversations

Navigating hard conversations can be challenging, but it is an important skill to have in order to effectively communicate and resolve conflicts. Here are some strategies for successfully navigating hard conversations:

- Prepare in advance: Think about the purpose of the conversation, the points you want to make, and potential objections or counterpoints. Write them down if necessary.
- Stay calm and composed: Keep your emotions in check and maintain a professional and respectful tone.
- Listen actively: Listen to the other person's perspective and try to understand their point of view.
- Speak honestly and directly: Be clear and honest in your communication and avoid being vague or evasive.
- Avoid blame and accusations: Focus on the problem or issue at hand, rather than placing blame or making accusations.

- Use "I" statements: Express your own thoughts and feelings, rather than making assumptions about the other person.
- Be open-minded: Be willing to consider new ideas and perspectives and be open to finding a compromise or solution.
- Find common ground: Look for areas of agreement and use them as a starting point for the conversation.
- Follow up: After the conversation, follow up to ensure that any actions or agreements made during the conversation are being implemented.

It's important to remember that hard conversations are a normal part of any relationship and can lead to growth and understanding if handled correctly.

How to Maintain Trust After a Hard Conversation

Maintaining trust after a hard conversation can be challenging for school-based leaders, staff members, and parents, but it is an important step in maintaining a positive and productive relationship. Here are some strategies for maintaining trust after a hard conversation:

- Follow through on commitments: If any agreements or actions were made during the conversation, make sure to follow through on them in a timely manner.

- Apologize if necessary: If any mistakes or misunderstandings occurred during the conversation, apologize for them and take responsibility for your actions.
- Keep the lines of communication open: Encourage open and honest communication, and make sure that any future issues or concerns are addressed in a timely manner.
- Show empathy: Show that you understand the other person's perspective and feelings and make an effort to see things from their point of view.
- Be transparent: Be open and honest about your thoughts, feelings and intentions.
- Demonstrate consistency: Be consistent in your actions, words and behaviors, as this will help to build trust over time.
- Reflect on your own actions: Take time to reflect on your own actions and consider how you can improve your communication and relationship-building skills.
- Show appreciation: Show appreciation for the other person's trust and willingness to engage in the hard conversation and express your willingness to continue to work together.

Remember, rebuilding trust takes time and effort, but it is worth it in the long run as it will help to strengthen the relationship.

Reflection Questions

1. Describe a difficult decision you have recently made. What went well and what would you change?

The Principal's Journey

2. How do you build consensus among your team members and move them towards a shared goal or vision?

The Principal's Journey

3. Think of the hardest professional conversation you have ever experienced. How did you maintain trust after the conversation?

The Principal's Journey

Chapter Nine: Time Management and Achieving a Work-Life Balance

Time management is crucial for school-based administrators to master, as it allows them to effectively allocate their time and resources towards their many responsibilities. With a limited amount of time, it is essential for principals to prioritize tasks, delegate duties, and make the most of their day. Good time management skills also ensure that deadlines are met, important tasks are not neglected, and that the school runs as smoothly as possible. Effective time management also allows principals to attend to the needs of students, staff, and parents, and to make time for personal and professional development. By managing their time well, administrators can create a positive work-life balance and be more productive in their role.

Poor time management can have significant negative impacts on overall productivity. First, it leads to procrastination and missed deadlines, which can result in decreased quality of work and decreased credibility. Next, disorganized work habits and constantly switching tasks can cause more stress and eventual burnout, leading to less motivation and creativity. Third, poor time management can lead to the misallocation of resources, resulting in wasted time, effort and funds. Poor time management skills can cause conflict with colleagues and stakeholders, who may become frustrated with missed commitments, ineffective communication, or delayed results as well. Lastly, poor time management can lead to an inability to prioritize and focus on the most important tasks, which can result in reduced productivity. To maintain high levels of leadership success in schools, it is important for principals to develop and maintain good time management skills.

Managing time effectively can be a challenge for school administrators, as they have to balance multiple responsibilities, meet deadlines, and attend to the needs of students, staff, and families. Some of the major challenges associated with time management within a school include:

- Significant Interruptions: Unplanned interruptions, such as impromptu meetings or unexpected student behavior, can disrupt a carefully planned daily schedule.
- Multitasking: School administrators often have to juggle multiple tasks at the same time, which can lead to reduced overall productivity.
- Lack of control over schedules: The school calendar, such as holidays and assessments, can impact the available time for certain tasks.

- Unclear priorities: With many tasks to complete, it can be difficult to determine which ones are the most important and should take priority.
- Distractions: Technology and other distractions can make it challenging to stay focused and on task.

To overcome these challenges, school administrators should set clear priorities, delegate tasks, and use time-management tools and strategies to ensure they make the most of their time. Principals can improve their time management skills through several methods:

- Prioritize tasks: Review your to-do list and prioritize tasks based on importance and urgency.
- Use a calendar: Use a calendar to schedule appointments, meetings, and deadlines to help you stay organized and on track.
- Delegate tasks: Delegate tasks to your assistant principal or other competent staff members to help lighten your workload.
- Take breaks: Make sure to take regular breaks throughout the day to refresh your mind and avoid burnout.
- Use technology: Utilize technology such as task management apps and digital calendars to help streamline your work.

- Set goals: Set clear, measurable goals for yourself and your team to help focus your efforts and stay motivated.
- Learn to say no: Learn to say no to non-essential tasks and requests to help manage your time more effectively.
- Eliminate distractions: Eliminate distractions such as social media to help you focus on your work.
- Focus on one task at a time: Multitasking can be counter-productive, try to focus on one task at a time.
- Reflect and review: Reflect on your day and review what worked well and what didn't in order to help you improve your time management skills over time.

The Importance of Rest

Resting and recharging are essential for maintaining good physical and mental health. When we take time to rest and recharge, we are giving our bodies and minds the opportunity to recuperate from the demands of daily life. This can help us feel refreshed, rejuvenated and better able to handle the challenges that we face. One of the most important benefits of resting and recharging is that it can help improve physical health. Getting enough sleep and rest can help reduce the risk of heart disease, obesity, and diabetes, by promoting physical healing, and repair of the body. Furthermore, regular rest and recharge can improve our emotional well-being, making us better able to cope with stress and maintain a positive attitude.

Resting and recharging also play a crucial role in increasing productivity. When we are well-rested and have had a chance to recharge, we are better able to focus and be productive at work. This means that taking time to rest and recharge can actually help us achieve more in the long run. Moreover, taking time to rest and recharge can help prevent burnout, which is a state of emotional, physical and mental exhaustion caused by excessive and prolonged stress. This is particularly important for principals who work long hours and have demanding jobs, as it can help them avoid the negative consequences of burnout, such as decreased productivity, poor health, and even depression. In addition, resting and recharging can help improve relationships. When we are well-rested and have had a chance to recharge, we are better able to be present and engaged with loved ones, which can improve our interpersonal relationships. Furthermore, when we take time to relax and recharge, we give our brains a chance to process information and come up with new ideas, which can boost creativity.

In conclusion, resting and recharging are essential for maintaining balance in our lives and to avoid overworking ourselves. It can help us improve physical and mental health, increase productivity, prevent burnout, improve relationships and boost creativity. Therefore, it is important to make time for rest and recharge on a regular basis.

Here are some tips to help you achieving a sustainable work life balance:

- Set boundaries: Set clear boundaries between work and personal time and stick to them.
- Prioritize self-care: Make time for activities that nourish your body and mind, such as exercise, meditation, and spending time with loved ones.
- Use time management techniques: Use techniques such as prioritizing tasks, delegating tasks, and managing distractions to make the most of your time.
- Communicate with your colleagues: Be transparent with your staff about your need for a sustainable work-life balance and encourage them to do the same.
- Learn to say no: It's important to set limits and say no to activities and requests that will take away from your personal time.
- Make time for hobbies and interests: Having hobbies and interests outside of work can help you relax, recharge and reduce stress.

- Unplug and disconnect: Disconnecting from work-related communication and technology during personal time can help you fully relax and recharge.
- Review and Reflect: Regularly review your schedule and reflect on whether you are achieving the balance you desire and make any necessary adjustments.

Reflection Questions

1. What challenges have you experienced with time management in your current position? How can you address them?

Dr. Rachel Edoho-Eket

2. List three (3) time management tools that work best for you, and list one additional strategy you would like to try in the coming month to help improve your productivity.

3. School-based leaders must prioritize their well-being and work-life balance. After reviewing the list of suggestions, write down one strategy that you will commit to.

Chapter Ten: Conclusion

Reflections on the Journey to Becoming a Principal

The journey to become a school-based leader is often filled with twists, turns, and winding roads. If you were to ask a group of administrators to collectively share their leadership stories, you would quickly see that no two journeys progressed in the same way. For me, my journey seemingly started with the initial question from my former principal inquiring about my future educational career plans, but in hindsight, my leadership journey was actually occurring for many years before I even realized that I was laying a foundation for school-based leadership.

Very early in my career as I entered my second year of teaching, I was devastated to learn that my classroom teacher position was surplused and I would have to seek a position at a different school. I truly loved my first school- the staff and students were warm and welcoming, I was just gaining my footing in my new role, and the parents embraced me as a trusted teacher. I reluctantly started the process of interviewing with other principals to find a new position and was offered the opportunity of a lifetime to open a new school in September of that year. In late July however, I received a phone call from my first principal sharing that I had a chance to return to my beloved school. My decision was complicated.

I wondered, should I stay in a familiar school that I was comfortable in, or should I go to a different school community and experience the unknown?

Take Opportunities as They are Presented

Taking calculated risks and seizing opportunities as they are presented to you is essential for your personal and professional growth. When individuals take calculated risks, they open themselves up to new opportunities for growth and development. Without taking risks, there is little development, as new ideas and experiences often come from exploring uncharted territory. The willingness to take risks is closely related to success, and those who take chances are more likely to achieve their goals and succeed in their endeavors. While there is always some degree of uncertainty and potential for failure associated with taking on new opportunities, the benefits far outweigh the costs. Furthermore, even failures can be valuable lessons that help you to grow and improve. In essence, taking risks and building upon new opportunities provides individuals with the chance to expand their abilities, reach their goals, and achieve success.

My final decision was to accept the opportunity to open a new school, and I am forever grateful for that decision. The new principal offered me several exciting leadership experiences including serving as a mentor teacher and participating in a small cohort of teachers that interfaced with the Superintendent on a quarterly basis to provide feedback. These two experiences dramatically increased my networking abilities and expanded my initial interest in school-based leadership. Later, those previous experiences would springboard me to my future position as an Instructional Team Leader opening a second new school in the district six years later. During my time at that school, my principal took an active mentorship role in my life and engaged me with many new opportunities designed to expand my visibility on a system-wide scale. In my proudest professional moment, I served on a discussion panel alongside other teacher leaders, our Superintendent, the State Superintendent, and the United States Secretary of Education!

Everything is an Interview

I have come to learn that everything you do, both professionally and personally, can be considered an interview. Every interaction you have with others, whether it is a job interview, a meeting, or even just a casual conversation with a colleague, can influence the way others perceive you and your leadership abilities. It is important to always be aware of this and to put your best foot forward in every situation. This includes being polite, professional, and articulate, as well as dressing appropriately and maintaining good body language. By being mindful of the image you are presenting to others, you can increase your chances of success in your professional life. As a classroom teacher I wore high heels every day. This was not only my style preference, but also helped me to feel positive at work. Sometimes, a few colleagues questioned me about my attire, but I simply smiled and shared that when I looked good, I felt good.

To make the best impression, it's important to be prepared, dress well, and to exhibit professional conduct. Before a meeting or interaction, it is a good idea to research any necessary information and to have a clear understanding of the purpose of the meeting. During the meeting, be polite and professional by greeting others warmly, maintaining good eye contact, speaking clearly, and showing a genuine interest in what others have to say. Confidence is also important, and you can exude it through your posture, body language, and communication skills. By following these tips, you can put your best foot forward and increase your chances of making a positive impression on everyone around you, including like-minded aspiring leaders.

The Importance of Aligning with other Strong Leaders

Aligning with other aspiring teacher leaders is a critical aspect of achieving success. By working closely with teachers who share similar goals, individuals can grow together while working towards a common objective. This collaboration can lead to better decision making as leaders can pool their resources, knowledge, and expertise to make informed choices. The credibility of a school-based project can also be improved by having stronger teacher leaders on board, as their reputation and influence can lend credibility to the initiative. Finally, aligning with other strong leaders can increase your impact, enabling the group to reach a wider audience and have a greater impact on the school community or district. I am extremely thankful for the teacher leaders who I worked alongside and continue to connect with through my journey to the principalship. We challenge each other to be better and provide a supportive network. I encourage you to partner with other strong leaders as you advance in your professional career.

Final Words of Encouragement for Future School Leaders

Being a school leader is a challenging and rewarding role that requires a strong commitment to the field of education and a heartfelt passion for student success. Here are my final words of advice and encouragement for future school leaders:

- Embrace the challenge: Being a school leader can be challenging, but it is also an incredibly rewarding experience. Embrace the challenges and use them as opportunities to grow and learn.

- Stay current on education trends and best practices: Stay informed about new research, policies, and best practices in education, and be willing to adapt and innovate in order to improve student learning outcomes and achievement.
- Build strong relationships: Building strong relationships with students, teachers, parents, and community members is essential for school leaders. Strong relationships are key to creating a positive and inclusive school culture and promoting student success.
- Be a lifelong learner: Being a school leader requires ongoing learning and professional development. Pursue advanced degrees and certifications, attend professional development opportunities and read professional journals to stay current and continue to grow as a leader.
- Lead by example: Lead by example, set high expectations for yourself and others, and hold yourself and others accountable for achieving them. Your actions and decisions should align with your school's mission and values.
- Empower others: Empower students, teachers, and staff to be active participants in creating a positive and inclusive school culture and promoting student success.

- Keep everything in perspective. Mistakes will happen and that is just fine. Apologize, correct the error quickly, and learn for the future.
- Find the joy in the role. Connect with people who make you smile and laugh at least once a day.

Being a school-based leader is a rewarding career, and the work you do can have a lasting impact on the lives of your future students, staff, and community members. If you are committed to making a positive difference in the lives of young people and have a passion for education and leadership, becoming a principal is the right choice for you. I wish you the best as you continue along your leadership path. Thank you for the meaningful contributions and life-changing work you will accomplish in your school communities!

Reflection Questions

1. Name one calculated risk or opportunity that you have taken over the course of your career. How did it help you to grow?

___
___
___
___
___
___
___
___
___
___
___
___
___
___
___
___
___
___
___
___

2. Who are the strong leaders that you align yourself with? If you do not have any yet, what steps can you take to network and interface with more leaders?

_____
_____
_____
_____
_____
_____
_____
_____
_____
_____
_____
_____
_____
_____
_____
_____
_____
_____
_____
_____

The Principal's Journey

3. Now that you have completed this book, create a timeline and short/long term plan for how you will transition into your next leadership role. Consider including key leadership experiences you still need, any skills to further develop, and certifications you need to finish.

_____
_____
_____
_____
_____
_____
_____
_____
_____
_____
_____
_____
_____
_____
_____
_____
_____
_____
_____

The Principal's Journey

About the Author

Dr. Rachel Edoho-Eket is a wife, mother, principal, public speaker, and author. With decades as a teacher and leader in public education, she has earned the reputation as a strong instructional leader, passionate educational advocate, and dedicated mentor. As the Principal of a top ranked school in Maryland, she is a life-long learner who strives for excellence not only for herself, but also for everyone she serves. Dr. Edoho-Eket's belief in fostering meaningful relationships serves as the foundation for everything she does, and her highly effective teaching and leadership style continues to inspire up and coming aspiring teacher leaders. During her educational career, she has proudly served as a classroom teacher, instructional team leader, mentor teacher, Assistant Principal, and Principal. Her book, "The Principal's Journey: Navigating the Path to School Leadership" provides a helpful and practical blueprint for educators to follow as they transition into new leadership roles.

Dr. Edoho-Eket holds a B.S. in Early Childhood and Elementary Education from Temple University, a M.S. in Curriculum and Instruction from McDaniel College, and a Doctorate in Leadership and Professional Practice from Trevecca Nazarene University.

www.ingramcontent.com/pod-product-compliance
Lightning Source LLC
Chambersburg PA
CBHW051944160426
43198CB00013B/2296